PRACTICAL
MEDITATION
with Buddhist Principles

HINKLER
BOOKS

Author: Venerable Thubten Lhundrup
Creative Director: Sam Grimmer
Design: Katherine Power
Photography: Ned Meldrum

Special thanks to Peter Thomas for
making it all happen, and for special footage and images of the Dalai Lama.
Thank you to the Tara institute for the use of its facilities.

First published in 2004
by Hinkler Books Pty Ltd
17-23 Redwood Drive
Dingley Victoria 3172 Australia
www.hinklerbooks.com

© Hinkler Books Pty Ltd 2004

Printed and bound in China

HINKLER
BOOKS

ISBN 1 7412 1513 7

CONTENTS

BUDDHIST MEDITATION IN YOUR DAILY LIFE

MAKING THIS BOOK A MEDITATION

One way of using this book is to select a topic at random and use it as the basis of your meditation(s) for that day.

MEDITATING AT HOME

Meditation can be practised almost anywhere and you do not need much to practice; essentially a cushion or chair and a small table to rest a book on would be enough. It is helpful to dedicate a space for this purpose. Your meditation space should be comfortable, clean, tidy, quiet and isolated from distractions.

BE GENTLE ON YOURSELF

The most common experience for someone meditating for the first time is the realisation of how busy the mind is. It is not until we attempt to quieten the mind that we realise there is a continuous arising of thoughts, memories, sounds, physical sensations and visions.

This is what the Lamas call the 'monkey-mind'. Just like a monkey's mind, ours too is continually jumping from one object to the next. By understanding the current nature of your mind, you can begin to learn how to change it.

The success of meditation depends on many factors, including your state of mind before the meditation, stress level and physical tiredness. As a result, some sessions are better than others. Don't expect too much, especially to begin with. Even experienced meditators have bad days. Be patient. Be gentle on yourself.

LEADING A MEDITATIVE LIFE

While the ultimate aim of a Buddhist practitioner is the attainment of an enlightened or Buddha mind, one without suffering, there are more basic goals that must be achieved first.

In the Tibetan language, the word for meditation has to do with 'familiarisation'. Through meditation, you can familiarise your mind with beneficial states and thoughts. Thoughts such as assisting others, compassion, treating others equally and morality. You begin to realise that non-virtuous thoughts such as hatred, anger, greed and jealousy are not only destructive to the people you direct them at but also to yourself.

This can be a confronting experience for some. It need not be. The idea is not to give yourself a hard time when contemplating the less favourable aspects of your nature but to use the awareness to begin change and improvement. It can be a source of positive change and a happier life.

INCORPORATING BUDDHIST PRINCIPLES INTO YOUR DAILY LIFE

WHAT IS BUDDHISM?

A religion, a philosophy, discipline of the mind, a way of life. The Buddhist Path is a personal experience of achieving deep and long-lasting happiness by gaining wisdom and a mind free of negative emotions. This can only happen if we cultivate positive practices and realise the benefits of doing so. Meditation is an essential means of accomplishing this.

WHO IS BUDDHA?

Approximately 2,500 years ago in the foothills of the Himalayas, in what is now Nepal, Siddhartha Gautama was born. He became known as the Sage of the Sakyas. His father was the king of the Sakya clan.

Not recognised as being of divine origin but essentially an ordinary being who followed the 'Path' and eventually attained enlightenment, Siddhartha was predicted to be either a great world leader or an enlightened teacher of gods and men.

His father was keen for him to be a leader of the kingdom and so ensured that young Siddhartha was educated in traditional arts, sciences, and sports and protected from the realities of life outside the walls of the kingdom.

Siddhartha inevitably ventured out and saw sights that made his life of luxury seem empty. He became aware of old age, sickness and death. The sight of a simple monk who was at peace with the world despite not having all the luxuries sought after by most, inspired Siddhartha to find the origin of suffering and the means to overcome it.

It was the custom at the time for someone of his position to leave his family and home and pursue a spiritual path if they wished. At the age of twenty-nine Siddhartha did so and took up the life of an ascetic.

After some time and experiencing much hardship, Siddhartha realised the ascetic life was ultimately futile. Arriving in a town called Bodhgaya he began deep

meditation under a Bodhi tree. His mind became clear and still. He remembered the successive series of rebirths he had experienced. Siddhartha came to realise that our lack of awareness of the true nature of reality causes the cycle of suffering known as samsara. This ignorance, combined with a false sense of 'self', causes us to carry out actions that due to the laws of karma, result in further suffering or unhappiness.

Having attained these realisations through self-examination and reflection, his mind became totally free of negative emotions.

Siddhartha became known as Buddha – 'the awakened one'. Shakyamuni Buddha is recognised as the Buddha of this age. There have been many before him and there will be many to follow.

DIFFERENT KINDS OF BUDDHISM

Since the 12th century, Buddhism has declined in India and currently accounts for just one per cent of its population. Despite this, Buddhism has, over the centuries, become an integral part of the spiritual, cultural and social aspects of many countries including China, Korea, Japan, Burma, Thailand, Cambodia, Vietnam, Sri Lanka, Central Asia, Tibet, Mongolia, Nepal, Bhutan and, more recently, throughout the West.

There are several forms of Buddhism, including:

THERAVADIN

The dominant form of Buddhism practised in southeast Asia, Theravadin has a lineage that began with the first followers of Buddha. Under the umbrella title of Theravadin, this type of Buddhism takes on many forms, depending on the particular country and its cultural influences.

In Thailand, for instance, there is a strong forest tradition where the practitioners live simple, secluded lives away from the towns and cities. This tradition has many Western followers and has been popularised by the work of masters such as Ajahn Chah. Theravadin is also practised in Sri Lanka, Myanmar (Burma), Laos, Kampuchea and Indonesia.

MAHAYANA/TANTRIC

Mahayana/Tantric Buddhism emphasises compassion for sentient beings as well as the concept of emptiness.

A bodhisattva (a practitioner who offers the merit he derives from good deeds to bring about the enlightenment of all sentient beings) possesses the innate tendency to become a Buddha. This disposition is believed to be inherent in all people.

The concept of emptiness does not deny the existence of phenomena but that they do not exist as we perceive them. Ignorance of this is a continuing cause of suffering for us.

From its origin in India, Mahayana/Tantric Buddhism spread to Central Asia, China, Japan, mainland Southeast Asia, Java, Sumatra, and Sri Lanka.

ZEN/JAPANESE/CHINESE/KOREAN

Tradition accepts that Buddha gave the first 'Zen' teaching in front of a large group of followers. After sitting in silence for some time, Buddha simply held up a flower for all to see. One disciple by the name of Mahakashyapa understood what had taken place. Words were no substitute for the flower.

The direct transmission from teacher to student has been the focus of Zen Buddhism since its beginnings in China in approximately AD500.

Two schools remain in existence today in Japan. The Soto School emphasises two main points, that there is no gap between enlightenment and practice and, secondly, that the correct behaviour is Buddhism itself. The Rinzai School is renowned for its use of koans or discussions between master and pupil.

By means of the basic practice of za-zen or sitting mediation, Zen aims at purifying and transforming the consciousness, ultimately realising the mind of a Buddha.

PURE LAND/CHINESE/JAPANESE

For any Buddhist practitioner, the state of mind at the time of death is considered to be extremely important. A negative state of mind can throw one into a rebirth of suffering, while a positive state will throw one into a higher form of rebirth.

For Pure Land devotees, the state of mind will, if suitable, result in rebirth in a Pure Land (Sukhavati) and beyond that only one more lifetime will need to be experienced before attaining liberation or Nirvana.

A MEDITATION

Following is a simple breathing meditation taught by the Buddha. By placing your thought on the breath, it is possible to quieten the 'monkey-mind' and improve concentration.

The aim is to become aware of the breath as it enters and leaves your body by concentrating on the rise and fall of the abdomen or the sensation of the breath passing through your lips or nostrils.

With the exhalation of each breath, count one, two, three, etc. Set yourself an achievable target of say seven to begin with. When sensations of quietness, stillness and peace eventually occur, hold them as best you can and experience them as fully as possible. When you are distracted or lose that sensation, return to the breath.

HOW TO HANDLE DISTRACTIONS

Distractions come in many forms. Sounds, visions, physical sensations such as pain in the knees or an itch, happy or unhappy memories, memories of people and events that you have not thought about for ages.

If you find that you are distracted easily, do not get angry or frustrated. This is the nature of the 'monkey-mind' and an awareness of this nature is actually a sign of progress.

The best way to handle these distractions is to not indulge them or attempt to repel them. As they arise in your mind, they will also disappear of their own accord. Simply acknowledge them and return the thought to the breath and resume counting.

BE PATIENT

As a patient mother will gently bring a curious, crawling baby back on to the blanket, we should be the same with our mind when it wanders. Patiently and gently bring it back to the breath, understanding that wandering or distraction is part of its current nature.

DON'T TRY TOO HARD

While effort is important, it is possible to try too hard to meditate. Meditation should be an enjoyable, inspiring experience. Ideally, you should be looking forward to the next meditation session and not feeling that it is a chore, finding reasons to avoid it. If you find yourself becoming frustrated at an apparent lack of success, it may be best to take a break. Go for a walk. Get some fresh air. Try again later in the day.

TEACHINGS OF THE BUDDHA

THE FOUR NOBLE TRUTHS

I SUFFERING EXISTS

Suffering exists in many forms. Some forms of suffering are plainly obvious and easily observed; others exist in very subtle ways and are not generally recognised.

If we are honest with ourselves, we will recognise that even at our happiest times a basic anxiety exists.

II THERE IS A CAUSE OF SUFFERING

Unless we address our basic unawareness of the true nature of life and our own existence, we will continue in the cycle of suffering. Once we have acknowledged a problem then determined its cause, we are able to take steps to eliminate it.

III SUFFERING CAN BE STOPPED

If we understand the cause of suffering or unhappiness, then we can take steps to remove that cause. We will then no longer experience the negative results. Unhappiness is not permanent, it comes and goes depending on conditions. For example, if we are expecting something pleasant to happen and it doesn't, we feel let down. This disappointment is dependent on our expectations, the conditions we created due to our desire. If suffering were independent then it would always remain unchanged.

IV THE PATH

The Buddhist Path contains methods for identifying the causes of unhappiness and removing them. The basic cause is fundamental ignorance or unawareness of the ultimate nature of reality. Wisdom is an antidote to this ignorance.

To develop this wisdom we need a better understanding of our mind and to put Buddha's teachings into practice. The path of developing this wisdom leads to peace and freedom from both suffering and unhappiness. Meditation is an essential part of this development.

THE NOBLE TRUTH OF SUFFERING

We are very good at denying or avoiding the reality that suffering exists. As long as this is the case, we will never overcome it. By accepting and confronting the fact that suffering exists, we can begin to determine the causes. By understanding the causes, we are then able to determine the appropriate action that will eliminate them.

Some forms of suffering are obvious: sickness, old age, death, war, famine and violence. Hatred, depression, fear, jealousy, desire etc. are also forms of suffering that, at the very least, disturb our mind and cause unhappiness. A more subtle form of suffering also exists, a basic anxiety or dissatisfaction with the volatile and imperfect nature of life. Regardless of happiness we may experience, the reality of life never lives up to our expectations.

When we acknowledge that suffering exists, we should not deny that happiness also exists. Generally, however, our experience of happiness is that it is short-lived and can never live up to our expectations. The sources of happiness we spend so much of our lives pursuing are never capable of providing that which we expect from them, lasting and profound happiness.

His Holiness the Dalai Lama has a profound understanding of the Four Noble Truths and suffering. From his own experience and that of his fellow Tibetans, he has become familiar with suffering but never seems to be overwhelmed by it. His Holiness would seem to be content, happy and is a wonderful example for us, showing that lasting happiness is possible but not from the usual sources we look to.

SUFFERING HAS A CAUSE

In a sense, our perception of our own existence becomes the point of reference for what we consider will make us happy or unhappy. We tend to think of ourselves as a solidly existing entity and all our experiences existing separately from our 'selves'. As a result, we pursue that which we feel makes the 'self' happy and avoid that which makes it unhappy.

We desire and become attached to relationships, possessions, lifestyle, etc., becoming depressed and anxious if we are not able to obtain them or we lose them. We also avoid that which we feel will make us unhappy (enemies, lack of resources, difficult situations) and become frustrated, angry, or hateful if we are unable to avoid them.

That which we wish for and that which we experience are more often than not vastly different.

Of course things such as material wealth, comforts and relationships can be sources of happiness and there is no reason we should not enjoy them if they are part of our lives. The problem arises when we become so dependent on them for our peace of mind and happiness that we are overwhelmed by emotions such as anger, sorrow, depression and anxiety when we lose them. Our peace of mind is then shattered and, as a result, we may act badly, hurting others and also ourselves by creating the causes for more unhappiness in the future.

IGNORANCE

Due to ignorance we perceive not only ourselves as existing independently from everything and everyone else but also we perceive objects, other people, situations and emotions in the same way.

We then determine these 'self-existing' phenomena as pleasant or unpleasant, good or bad, suffering or happiness.

As a result of wishing to experience happiness and to avoid suffering we develop attachment or aversion towards those phenomena.

Thoughts and actions based on attachment or aversion result in negative seeds of karma in our mindstream. On ripening, these seeds cause us to continue the cycle.

STOPPING SUFFERING

'If only I could fix the world, people and events so they were the way I want them to be then everything would be all right. Then I really would be happy!' How often have you felt that way?

It is unrealistic to expect things to be like that, and, when we do, we create suffering for ourselves. Yet many people live their whole life with that wish in mind, endlessly pursuing it, becoming frustrated, angry, depressed when it never works out. It is easier and more skilful to 'fix' your own mind; the rest will then follow.

It can be encouraging to consider that the Buddha was once like we are now. Buddha assures us through his teaching, that an enlightened mind, a mind 'awakened' to the true nature of reality is possible. It is in fact already there!

Imagine a mirror. When the mirror is clean, without any blemishes to obscure the image, it has the quality to reflect accurately. If it is dirty then it is no longer able to accurately reflect the image but the quality that allows it to do so is still there, it has not gone, it is just obscured. In the same way, our mind has this quality, it has always been there, it is just obscured by the 'dirt' of wrong perceptions. If we, like the Buddha, clean away the obstructions, we will expose the true nature of our mind. Our own enlightened mind. Our Buddha mind, reflecting the true undistorted nature of reality.

With a more accurate perception of the nature of the 'self', our experiences and also acceptance and understanding of the transitory nature of life comes a deep feeling of peace and contentment.

The happiness that results from this type of mind is not affected by outside phenomena and is more durable and dependable than the unstable, ever-changing happiness that we experience from the usual sources.

THE WAY TO STOP SUFFERING

There is a definite path leading to the end of suffering. If we are able to rid our minds of the ignorance or incorrect perception of the reality of our 'selves' and all other phenomena, then we will be able to determine which actions we should abandon and those we should practise.

Suffering will continue as long as we ignorantly carry out actions based on a concept of our 'self' as being totally independent or self-existing. These actions produce results that will be in the form of suffering.

By developing wisdom and an understanding of how the cycle of suffering perpetuates, we can ultimately stop the cycle, stop the suffering and achieve enlightenment.

A MEDITATION

Begin with a few minutes of breathing meditation as described earlier.

As best you can relive the day so far. From the moment you woke up to the present. Consider each action you carried out. Not just the big, more significant actions but all the smaller ones as well.

Possibly the first action had to do with staying in bed for just five more minutes or the desire to get to the kitchen for breakfast. Maybe there was a disturbing thought of things that had to be done at work or a pleasant thought of having lunch with a friend.

What other thoughts and actions occurred as the day progressed? Impatience or even anger when you had to wait in a queue at the bank? Satisfaction when you drove into the last parking space before someone else? Bitterness when you realised you had to spend the day with someone you did not like? Delighted when your boss praised you in front of others?

If we are honest with ourselves, we will see that our day is filled with thoughts and actions that are directed at avoiding suffering in its many forms and experiencing happiness. This is a motivation common to all sentient beings, the wish to experience happiness and avoid suffering.

There is, of course, no problem with possessions, wealth, a comfortable lifestyle etc. The real problem is our underlying belief that these things will make us truly happy. Forever!

Consider a time when you saved up and worked hard for something, made sacrifices and practised patience until it was possible to finally obtain the object of your dreams. Where is that object now, what significance does it play in your life, do you still regard it with the same sentiment? Chances are that you have moved on to other objects of desire.

Think again of a previous object of desire, a relationship, or even a situation. If at the time we knew what we know now, that it was impermanent and had no chance of living up to our expectations would we have suffered so much to obtain it? Would we have placed such importance on it/them? Would we have become so overwhelmed by the thought of having to have it/them otherwise our life would be ruined?

Finish the meditation by considering ways in which you may be able to understand the impermanent nature of phenomena in your life. Appreciating them in a more rational way can prevent the extremes of attachment and desire or aversion and anger.

Consider the peace and contentment that would create in your mind.

THE EIGHTFOLD NOBLE PATH

Developing the wish to be free from samsara, free from suffering altogether, the practitioner can observe the Eightfold Noble Path. This path becomes the basis for achieving a liberated mind, the state of Nirvana. Observing these can also be an effective guide to every-day behaviour for non-Buddhists.

The Eightfold Noble Path incorporates Right View, Right Intention, Right Speech, Right Action, Right Livelihood, Right Effort, Right Mindfulness, and Right Concentration.

THE THREE HIGHER TRAININGS - ETHICS, MEDITATION AND WISDOM

Observing ethics or morality stops negative actions that, due to the certainty of karma, will result in more suffering; actions of body, speech and mind that are not only harmful to us but others as well. Wisdom is not possible without meditation and effective meditation is not possible without ethics.

In meditation it is possible to transform mere intellectual or academic knowledge into realisations, deep and profound understanding related to ones own experience.

To attain these states and then clean the 'mirror' of the mind, we need to also practise morality to lead an ethical life. By doing so, we are more able to destroy the habits of greed, ignorance and hatred.

Wisdom is gained by hearing, learning, contemplating and thinking but most importantly by meditating. Through meditation we overcome the ignorance or incorrect perception of our 'self' and of all phenomena.

While many Buddhists take vows in relation to certain practices ranging from a brief list of non-virtuous actions to ordination and tantric vows, such guidelines regarding ethics and morality can be beneficial for Buddhists and non-Buddhists alike.

Being in the Mahayana tradition, Tibetan Buddhism encompasses all these aspects or categories of practice in the Six Perfections – namely Generosity, Ethical Discipline, Patience, Perseverance or Joyful Effort, Meditative Concentration and Wisdom. The life or practice of a Bodhisattva is based on these Six Perfections.

Bodhisattvas or 'heroes of enlightenment' are beings who, out of great compassion, dedicate their lives to the attainment of enlightenment not just for themselves but for the sake of all sentient beings. Their wish is to remain in cyclic existence to benefit sentient beings.

Developed to the point of being beyond just practices but becoming perfections and carried out with great compassion for all sentient beings these are the means of attaining the enlightened mind of a Buddha.

THE TEN NON-VIRTUOUS ACTIONS

As discussed earlier, leading an ethical life is the basis of Buddhist practice. At the very least the Ten Non-Virtuous Actions should be avoided and their opposites adopted. This top ten list can also be a beneficial reference for non-Buddhists who wish to lead a more ethical life.

Of course there is an infinite variety of ways that these actions may be carried out. The ten presented can be seen as major categories of possible negative actions of body, speech and mind.

ACTIONS OF BODY
Killing
Stealing
Sexual Misconduct

ACTIONS OF SPEECH
Lying
Divisive Speech
Harsh Words
Meaningless Talk/Gossip

ACTIONS OF MIND
Covetousness
Ill-will
Wrong View

The most important element in any action is the motivation. If we kill with hatred, the resulting karma will be extremely strong and result in great suffering in the future. If we kill with the motivation of mercy, compassion or with regret, the resulting karma will still be negative but not as severe.

The object of an action can also be influential in the strength of the karma produced. Any action directed at holy objects or holy people results in strong karmic consequences. This also applies to actions directed at our parents, as they were a fundamental part of the conditions that resulted in our human rebirth and showed great kindness to us when we were young. Human rebirth is the best for the practice of Dharma and holds the possibility of enlightenment in a lifetime.

MEDITATION ON THE TEN NON-VIRTUOUS ACTIONS

When meditating on these actions it is extremely important to avoid feelings of guilt regarding past actions. Guilt is destructive and plays no part in the practice of Bhudda's teachings. Developing what may be called intelligent regret can be beneficial. We need to accept that we have faults and are not perfect. By contemplating past actions and the associated motivations, we can intelligently admit that we were not so skilful, but given a similar situation in the future we now have the insight to act differently.

To stop negative actions is beneficial, but to take the further step of avoiding committing them in the future is more so. To then take up the opposite, positive actions, is extremely skilful and beneficial, resulting in not only less suffering in the future but also creating the causes for great happiness.

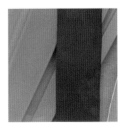

MEDITATIONS

We all wish for happiness and to be free from suffering but this desire is no better than that of an animal if we do not develop an understanding of our mind and be mindful of our thoughts, words and actions.

By meditating, a Buddhist practitioner's ultimate aim is enlightenment, but anyone can benefit greatly from regular practice. Then, when the experiences and realisations of meditating are taken beyond the cushion and into daily activities, the real application of Buddha's teachings takes place. This is when we and others benefit from our transformed actions.

For a beginner, regular and brief meditation sessions are more beneficial than occasional attempts at longer sessions. If we try to do too much too soon there is the chance of becoming disheartened, feeling that meditation is just a painful, frustrating experience.

1 Cross your legs if sitting on a cushion. Sitting on a chair is fine.

2 With your palms facing upwards, place your right hand on top of your left with the tips of your thumbs gently touching. Hands resting in your lap.

3 Hold your back comfortably straight, not so rigid that you experience discomfort or tension during the session.

4 Relax your jaw and allow your tongue to rest behind your front, top teeth.

5 Tilt your head slightly forward.

6 Your eyes may be closed, although this can increase the chance of falling asleep. If you have your eyes open, have them only slightly open, gazing downwards without focusing.

7 Hold your shoulders level and keep your elbows slightly away from your body.

Begin with a few minutes of breathing meditation as explained earlier.

Generate a positive motivation. This helps to clarify why you are making the effort to meditate.

At the end of the meditation dedicate the effort you have made and the resulting positive karma created as a result.

The first step in the session is to check your posture. The following seven points are widely accepted as being important as they help the subtle energies in the body flow freely and reduce the chances of distraction. They are not compulsory though. The main concern is to be comfortable to avoid moving around or being distracted by discomfort, but not too relaxed that you fall asleep or experience dullness.

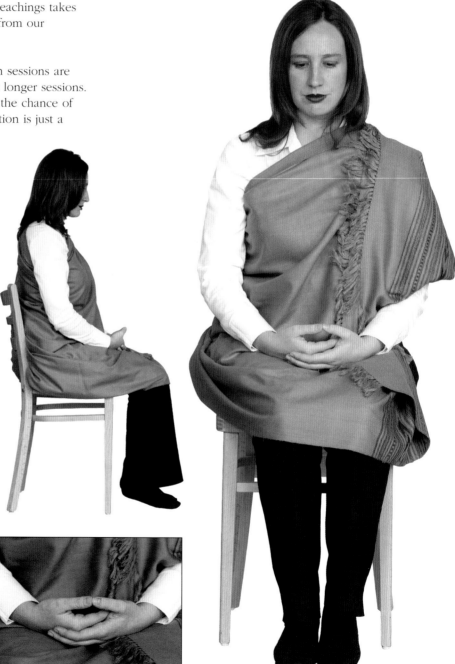

KILLING

Intentionally taking the life of another sentient being is considered one of the most harmful actions we can carry out.

Sentient beings include humans, animals, insects, birds and fish. Sentient beings value their lives above anything else. The inability of non-human beings to express that thought in words does not diminish the fact that they all wish to live and not to die.

The process of reincarnation causes our mental continuum to experience all manner of rebirth states. The human rebirth is recognised as being extremely rare and, for that reason, taking the life of a human is most severe in its karmic consequences.

Killing without intention, accidentally or unknowingly is a very different situation than taking a life with a motivation of hatred, desire or ignorance. If we inadvertently kill a sentient being, the karmic results will be much lighter than if we were to carry out the action deliberately.

A MEDITATION

Contemplate that all sentient beings are just like us in that they cherish their life above all else and wish to be happy. Consider that the causes of death in this world are many, without us contributing to them.

Think about times when you deliberately killed insects, fish or animals and recall your motivation at the time. Was there a feeling of anger, hatred or greed? Was the action carried out thoughtlessly without any concern for the suffering caused?

Apart from the suffering caused and the destroying of a sentient being's life, the karmic results of killing will be great suffering in future lives. Develop a sense of regret for causing suffering and creating the cause for future suffering for oneself.

Resolve to avoid killing when a similar situation occurs. Consider ways in which you may be able to protect and nurture life.

STEALING

Whether we take someone else's possession by force, deception, secretly or by borrowing and not giving back, the karma created by the action will result in some form of suffering for us in the future.

It may seem that some objects are too insignificant or will not be missed but if we are unable to cultivate the correct attitude in relation to small things then the chances are we will not be able to act correctly with regard to bigger, more significant objects.

Unfortunately, the actions of some business people these days are not at all helpful in setting an example for us. Getting away with what you can is sadly a widely accepted practice. By acting honestly we can influence family, friends and work colleagues and be of great benefit to them as well as ourselves.

A MEDITATION

Contemplate that material wealth is not a real source of happiness, especially when obtained by stealing. When we die, the only thing that will be able to help us is our mind. Material objects are impermanent and will be of no use.

Recall an incident when you may have stolen something of value and the possible motivations of greed or desire.

Develop a sense of regret for causing inconvenience to someone else and creating the causes for your own future suffering.

Resolve to avoid stealing when the opportunity presents itself again and to practise generosity towards others.

SEXUAL MISCONDUCT

Generally, sexual misconduct can be considered as any action of a sexual nature that causes suffering to another.

Sexual desire is strong so there is a need to be careful and avoid situations where we may carry out actions that turn out to be harmful to others and possibly result in disputes, anger and even violence. Given the right circumstances and a mind overwhelmed by desire, anger or affected by intoxicants the possibility of sexual misconduct is greater.

Rape, adultery, sex with another's partner, sex with children or prohibited family members are all obvious forms of sexual misconduct.

A MEDITATION

Contemplate that a disciplined mind is the basis for developing a peaceful, content life and, if uncontrolled, our mind will continue to bring suffering and dissatisfaction.

Recall an incident of sexual misconduct and consider the suffering caused as a result. Contemplate the motivation for the action.

Develop a sense of regret for causing harm and suffering.

Resolve to avoid similar actions in the future and especially the circumstances that may lead to those actions.

Reflect on ways you may contribute actively to loyalty in any relationship and cultivate trustworthiness.

LYING

Words are not always necessary to lie. Sometimes saying nothing at the right time or a simple gesture can be just the same as giving the incorrect impression through speech.

Lying also includes deception or manipulating the truth to suit the needs of creating the wrong understanding. Truth is often masked by the 'spin' put in place to justify actions.

Lying can also refer to written contracts or agreements where our signature indicates we agree to certain statements being true. If we know that this is not the case, or some of the statements are only partially true, we have carried out the action of lying.

A MEDITATION

Contemplate the suffering that is caused by lying and the possibility of being considered untrustworthy by others as a result.

Recall an incident where you deliberately acted to give someone the incorrect impression. What was the motivating factor?

Develop a sense of regret regarding the inconvenience caused.

Resolve to avoid lying, be truthful and cultivate trust in the minds of people that you deal with.

PRACTICAL MEDITATION · 29

DIVISIVE SPEECH

Any talk that deliberately contributes to disharmony between one or more parties is regarded as divisive speech.

Whether what is said is true or false does not matter if the intention is to create division or animosity. In the world of politics, for example, this practice is a common way of promoting distrust in the minds of the public.

Due to motivations such as anger or desire, one person may deliberately talk about another's partner and their failings. Even if the observations are true, this type of talk may help develop or reinforce negative feelings about that person, creating division between the two.

A MEDITATION

Contemplate that there are many causes for animosity, disagreements and hostility. Any action we carry out to contribute to this is a cause for more suffering.

Recall an incident when you contributed to disharmony between people.

Develop a sense of regret for contributing to ill feelings between people.

Resolve to avoid talk that creates divisions and to encourage tolerance, reconciliation and harmony whenever possible.

HARSH WORDS

Cruel words pointing out the faults of others can have long-term effects in the minds of the victims, especially young children who tend to believe what they are told.

Most of the time, harsh words or abuse are motivated by anger, but sarcastic words can also be hurtful.

Any talk that causes unhappiness or discomfort to another, even if spoken pleasantly, can be classed as the negative action of harsh words.

A MEDITATION

Contemplate the wish that all people have, to hear pleasant words, not harsh, angry or critical words.

Recall a time when you may have spoken harshly to someone. What was the motivation?

Develop a sense of regret for hurting or causing distress to the other person.

Resolve to avoid harsh words and to speak kindly, particularly when people may be vulnerable. Choose to praise not criticise.

MEANINGLESS TALK/GOSSIP

Gossip can be very common in the workplace where there is often resentment or jealousy between groups in a company. For example, between sales and creative departments or between managers and employees. It is often accepted practice to gossip about other departments or management. In this situation, the motivation may be just a wish to fit in with colleagues, but even then the conversations reinforce an 'us' and 'them' attitude.

Gossip arouses negative thoughts regarding others and generates negative states of mind in the people taking part in the conversation.

One incident of meaningless talk may seem to be just that, meaningless. But, if a mind becomes used to this sort of action due to repetition then it is said that even such a seemingly insignificant action will become extremely heavy in its karmic consequences. For a Buddhist practitioner, meaningless talk can be a great hindrance to spiritual progress.

A MEDITATION

Contemplate that engaging in meaningless talk contributes to an undisciplined mind and negative states can arise more easily.

Recall a time when you engaged in gossip.

Develop a sense of regret for having a lack of control over your mind.

Resolve to avoid gossip, to speak of meaningful and positive things that help bring happiness and benefit to you and others.

COVETOUSNESS

With a mind filled with greed, overly attached to possessions and the wish to have more, a person may think that the possessions, wealth, lifestyle or talents of others should be theirs.

There is nothing wrong with those objects in themselves but a mind filled with desire and greed will not be satisfied, despite how many are accumulated, and envy of those with more is easily aroused.

A MEDITATION

Contemplate how the covetous mind brings dissatisfaction and discontent.

Recall thoughts you may have had that fall into this category of covetousness or greed.

Develop a sense of regret for such thoughts.

Resolve to be generous towards others and to be content with what you have.

WRONG VIEW

For the Buddhist practitioner, wrong view and the act of killing are the worst of the negative actions.

Wrong view relates to three views in particular:

1 That the Law of Cause and Effect i.e. karma does not exist.

2 There is a permanent 'self', the belief of eternalism.

3 That there are no past or future lives and things arise spontaneously without cause, the belief of nihilism.

Buddha's teachings tell us that these views are the cause of great and continuing suffering. A mind with these views would not believe the remaining non-virtuous actions to be so harmful, resulting in them arising more easily.

A MEDITATION

Contemplate the suffering caused by a mind of self-cherishing. Consider the laws of karma and the possible causes for experiences you are going through.

Recall a time when you were overwhelmed by negative thoughts or emotions. Would it have been of benefit at that time to have some understanding as to why you were experiencing those thoughts?

Resolve to listen, think and meditate on ways of developing knowledge and wisdom

ILL-WILL

Jealousy, retribution, envy may all be motivations for wishing to harm others or see them suffer in some way, but ill-will can also be very deceptive.

The 'tall poppy' syndrome where satisfaction, however subtle, is experienced by seeing happy, talented or wealthy people falling from fame or fortune can be classed as a form of ill-will.

A MEDITATION

Contemplate on the fact that all sentient beings wish to be happy and avoid suffering, as you do yourself.

A mind thinking of ill-will towards others is never happy.

Recall a time when you may have wished misfortune on others or experienced a sense of satisfaction when others experienced suffering of some kind.

Develop a sense of regret for such thoughts and the suffering they cause for you in the future.

Resolve to be mindful of the fact that others are just like you, they also need love, compassion and protection.

BUDDHISM IN THE WEST

Today, 2,500 years after Shakyamuni Buddha attained enlightenment Buddhism accounts for just one per cent of the population in the country of its birth, India.

Since that time, however, it has spread to Asia, China, Japan, Korea and Tibet.

The majority of the populations in Thailand, Kampuchea, Myanmar, Bhutan, Sri Lanka, Laos and Vietnam are Buddhist.

A great Buddhist master of the 8th century, Padmasambhava, predicted that the Dharma would spread in the West 'when the iron bird flies and horses run on wheels'.

From the 19th century, Buddhism slowly came to be known to Westerners.

Zen, the Japanese branch of Buddhism, was popular amongst the 'beat generation' of the 1950s. Then, with the popularity of Eastern culture in the 1960s, various forms of Buddhism became more firmly established.

Since then, many masters have travelled to the West to teach and establish centres in Europe, North America, South America, South Africa and Australasia.

With growing disenchantment in established religions and the ability of people to access and learn about alternatives, Buddhism is experiencing considerable growth in many Western countries as it satisfies the thirst for spiritual nourishment.

LAMAS AND GURUS

The lama (Tibetan) or guru (Sanskrit) is of great significance in Tibetan Buddhism. As a practitioner's spiritual teacher, the lama is considered supreme as the object towards which the disciple can direct spiritual activity in mind and actions.

Providing a living role model of what can be attained through proper practice and seen as the Buddha by his disciple, the lama provides a means for the disciple to develop essential trust and to abandon attachment to worldly concerns.

For a proper and effective guru/disciple relationship, appropriate qualities are required from both the disciple and the teacher.

THE DALAI LAMA

Known to his fellow countrymen as Kundun or The Presence, His Holiness the Fourteenth Dalai Lama is the spiritual and temporal leader of Tibetans.

Following the death of the thirteenth Dalai Lama the traditional procedure of observation and examination took place. In 1937, Tenzin Gyatso a two-year-old boy from Amdo, a region in northeastern Tibet, was recognised as his reincarnation.

Tenzin Gyatso was educated in the usual religious subjects culminating in his attainment of a degree of Geshe (an academic title equivalent to a Doctorate in Western terms) at the age of twenty-five.

As a teenager, His Holiness took over the full responsibilities of his office due to political pressures and the impending occupation of Tibet by China. Despite repeated attempts at reconciliation, His Holiness was forced to leave his homeland in 1959. Since then, the Indian government has provided sanctuary in the town of Dharamsala.

Over 100,000 Tibetans have fled over the mountains to be near His Holiness and the numbers increase daily. Many refugees also live in Nepal, Bhutan and the West.

Despite the hardships suffered by himself and his fellow Tibetans at the hands of the Chinese Government, His Holiness has consistently advocated a policy of non-violence. In 1989, His Holiness was awarded the Nobel Peace Prize and continues to tour worldwide teaching Buddhist philosophy and promoting peaceful resolution as the only way to end conflict.

THE BUDDHIST WAY TO ENLIGHTENMENT

We are inclined to talk about our mind as something solid like a container, or maybe even a filing cabinet located in our head. We often say such things as: 'I'll keep it in mind', 'My mind is full of thoughts', etc. However, the mind is not a physical object. No matter how skilful a surgeon may be, they are unable to extract the mind from a body and hold it in their hands.

Buddha's teachings tell us that the mind is formless; a beginningless, endless, dynamic process of experiences that are continually arising. From beginningless time, our minds have been reincarnating and experiencing the various sufferings of samsaric existence. Our bodies in different states of existence act like vehicles for the mind.

As long as we are satisfied with this sort of existence and do nothing, it will continue. But by becoming aware of the nature and potential of our mind we can begin to understand that profound changes are possible.

The experiences that are currently arising and forming our mind are not doing so without cause. For something to exist or come into existence there must be a reason, a cause or action to create the effect. According to Buddhist beliefs, things do not 'just happen'.

These experiences are driven by karma, the Law of Cause and Effect. Our mind is a result of our past actions causing effects to arise now. Buddha observed and taught about the laws of karma, how certain actions result in experiences of suffering, while others result in experiences of happiness.

If we are able to modify our behaviour appropriately, understanding that certain actions bring certain results, then we can begin to create the causes for happiness in the future instead of suffering. To start, we need to develop an understanding of the nature of our mind then we will have an informed idea of what changes to make.

Buddha has shown us the way to do this by detailing the actions required and the ways we can create the conditions in our mind to allow those actions to arise naturally. While there may be a considerable delay between the action and

its karmic result, we can experience profound changes in our lives by modifying our actions.

A more peaceful mind, contentment, less worry, less stress and deeper happiness; all this is possible as well as a more profound love and appreciation for those close to us and for all sentient beings. A mind that looks at other sentient beings with compassion, love and care is one that will convert all our actions into a cause to attain Buddhahood, an enlightened mind. With this sort of mind our resulting actions will create happiness, not only for us but also those we come into contact with.

If the reverse is true then it is easy to see what the result would be – negative actions creating unhappiness and disharmony in our minds and in the minds of those we come into contact with. It is essential to be aware of our actions and understand their consequences.

The priceless and very precious positive state of mind is our responsibility to cultivate and maintain, as there are few sources of assistance from outside. The positive influences in our lives are greatly outnumbered by negative influences. In any given day our minds are exposed to an overwhelming amount of information via radio, television, newspapers, magazines, billboards and, of course, other people. Most of this information is not a positive influence for our minds. There is a need to be more discriminating with the input our minds receive, to minimise the harmful effects accumulated so easily.

The first step is awareness. Then the willingness and motivation to investigate, analyse and identify the positive or negative, constructive or destructive influences and states of mind.

This is not an easy process. It takes great effort to be diligent and maintain a virtuous mind. It is said it is not possible for a negative thought to be in our mind at the same time as a positive thought. Considering this, we need to consciously cultivate the positive thoughts and swamp the negative ones, outnumber them, rather than fighting them and getting frustrated when they dominate.

With the practice of meditation we can familiarise our mind with appropriate thoughts. Meditation also allows us to contemplate the teachings of Buddha and relate them to our own experience. This is the way to transform mere intellectual knowledge into profound, life-changing realisations.

With practice, meditation and a mind of compassion for others, we are doing more than just wishing peace, happiness and good conditions for others, we are also counteracting our own hatred, anger and negative states of mind.

MINDFULNESS

Our mind can be our own greatest enemy! Buddha taught that if control can be gained over the mind, then control will be gained over everything. The purpose of meditation in which we watch the breath was taught by Buddha to develop mindfulness.

In Buddhist terminology, mindfulness is that faculty of the mind that helps to maintain attention on an object of meditation. This ability is crucial in developing advanced levels of meditation where undistracted focus on an object for great lengths of time is necessary. Mindfulness in our everyday activities benefits us more immediately by contributing to a peaceful, stress-free mind.

From the moment we wake in the morning, we tend to follow the impulses of the 'monkey-mind' with occasional periods of taking control to focus on the task at hand. As a result, many actions are carried out subconsciously and we are unable to recall doing them.

You may have had the experience of driving to a destination, arriving, and then not being able to recall how you got there. While we may have times where we are focused on a task, more often than not we are thinking of other things.

Think of a recent face-to-face conversation you had with someone. What thoughts were going through your mind at the time? Were you really listening to the other person or just hearing part of what they said while busily thinking of other things?

Much of the time we are not really listening. We half hear then quickly make assumptions about what the person is saying and start to think of appropriate responses. It is not often that we really listen mindfully.

When we are physically ill we may be distracted by pain or discomfort resulting in our inability to carry out physical actions properly. So it is with our mind. Distracted by other thoughts, we are unable to concentrate on the task at hand. This can result in not doing tasks to the best of our ability. We may be doing the task to simply get it over and done with rather than doing it mindfully.

By practising mindfulness we can become discerning about the thoughts we let into our mind. More importantly, we can check our motivation for carrying out an action. What are the consequences of the action? Is it an action that will create happiness or suffering for others and myself? Is the action motivated by the thought of cherishing myself at the expense of others? Is there a more skilful way to handle this situation?

If we can develop mindfulness, we begin to take control of our mind rather than be controlled by it. Less stress, improved concentration and a feeling of more control over our lives are all possible if we make the effort but these really are only short-term benefits. For the Buddhist practitioner, mindfulness is a vital faculty of the mind to be developed as it is indispensable in achieving higher states of meditation.

THE CERTAINTY OF KARMA

One of the Laws of Karma states that a positive action will and can only produce a positive result while a negative action will and can only produce a negative result. The reverse is never possible. This is the certainty of karma.

Buddha did not place any moral judgement on these actions, he simply observed that according to the Laws of Karma they result in suffering for us in the future. The opposite of these actions, abandoning them and carrying out the opposing action, results in happiness.

TEN NON-VIRTUOUS ACTIONS

As discussed earlier in this book, Buddha specified ten precepts to observe. These are considered to be actions to avoid. There are, of course, many more than ten actions we should avoid. The ten listed in further detail here, are to be considered as major categories if you like; each represents many permutations and variations.

ACTIONS OF BODY

KILLING: taking the life of any sentient being is considered to be the most serious of the three actions of the body.

STEALING: taking something of value which has not been offered.

SEXUAL MISCONDUCT: engaging in sex with someone other than your partner or with someone else's partner, anyone who does not consent or with an improper person such as your sister, brother, parent or child.

ACTIONS OF SPEECH

LYING: deceiving someone by saying something you understand to be untrue. Of course you do not have to say anything at all to give someone the incorrect impression, the written word, gestures or even silence can qualify as the act of lying.

DIVISIVE SPEECH: the intention here is to divide two people or groups of people or to contribute to them being unable to resolve a conflict.

HARSH WORDS: directed at someone who understands and is hurt by what you say and how you say it.

MEANINGLESS TALK/GOSSIP: speaking about meaningless things while considering them to be important.

ACTIONS OF MIND

COVETOUSNESS: the wish to possess the belongings or qualities of someone else.

ILL WILL: wishing harm towards another person.

WRONG VIEW: this action of mind refers specifically to Buddhist principles. If you do not understand the Laws of Karma, for example, yet you hold definite negative opinions regarding it, this would be considered wrong view.

The karmic results of these actions is greatly influenced by the motivation involved and the consequences of each action. For example, if we carry out the action of harsh words but do so with positive motivation then the karmic result will not be as great as it would be if there were a motivation of hatred or anger.

By making the conscious decision to abandon these actions means we prevent the creation of negative karma. By carrying out actions that are the opposite of the non-virtuous actions we create positive karma.

For example, the opposite of stealing can be generosity or giving. If we give generously to someone who is in need, we create positive karma and the experience for us when that karma ripens or produces its effects will be a cause of happiness for us.

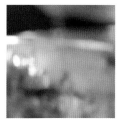

DAILY MEDITATION ON A SACRED PHRASE

The phrases overleaf may be used as suggested topics for meditation.

Begin by generating a thought of motivation for the meditation session. Following a period of breathing meditation, recite the selected phrase softly to yourself a number of times.

Consider the general meaning of the phrase. Then consider how the phrase relates to your experiences. It may relate directly to a personal weakness such as anger or it may help you understand the weakness of others. You may find, at first, that there is no obvious relevance to you but after contemplating different situations you have been in and people you have known you may find it shows there could have been more skilful ways of handling those situations.

After meditation on the topic and applying it to various experiences, consider how you can use your observations to make further actions of body, speech and mind more beneficial for yourself and the people you come in contact with.

At the end of the session, dedicate the positive karma created by the session to the enlightenment and freedom from suffering of all sentient beings.

While the verses may be quite useful as topics for meditation sessions, they can be very effective also as topics of contemplation throughout the day. This is also true for any of the teachings we may read or hear including the information in this book. The knowledge is really of no use unless we apply it, put it into action.

My suggestion would be to choose one topic per day for meditation and contemplation. Meditate on the topic at home on the cushion and then take the topic with you, contemplating it in differing circumstances, driving, on the train or bus, at work, dealing with people, shopping or having coffee with a friend.

Ask yourself: 'How does the topic relate to the situation I am in now? How could it help me deal with this situation, this person, this emotion?'.

By relating these phrases and the teachings to your own life, your own circumstances and experiences they become very effective in changing our thoughts and actions. If we don't meditate or contemplate them in this way they will be nothing more than nice sounding words. They will serve no other purpose.

PHRASES TO MEDITATE ON

How wonderful it would be if all sentient beings were to live in equanimity, free of hatred and attachment!
How wonderful it would be if all sentient beings had happiness and the causes of happiness!
How wonderful it would be if all sentient beings were free of suffering and its causes!
How wonderful it would be if all sentient beings were never separated from the happiness of higher rebirth and liberation!

The Four Immeasurable Thoughts

This day is a special day,
It is yours.
Yesterday slipped away
It cannot be filled with more meaning.
About tomorrow nothing is known.
But this day, today, is yours,
Make use of it.
Today you can make someone happy.
Today you can help another.
This day is a special day,
It is yours.

Indian poem

Nothing exists the way it appears, it is all up to our karma.

Padmasambhava

If you wish others to be happy, practise loving kindness.
If you wish to be happy, practise loving kindness.

His Holiness the Dalai Lama

Wisdom arises through effort, wisdom disappears through lack of effort; knowing this twofold path of growth and decline, one should arrange oneself such that wisdom increases.

The Buddha

It is easy to see the fault of others, hard to see one's own. One sifts the faults of others like chaff, but covers up one's own, as a crafty cheater covers up a losing throw.

The Buddha

Just as rust eats away the iron from which it is produced, so do their own deeds lead the overindulgent into a miserable state.

The Buddha

Phrases to Meditate On

(continued)

The wise who control body, speech and mind are indeed the consummately controlled.
                                    The Buddha

Speak the truth, do not become angered, and give when asked, even be it a little. By these three conditions one goes to the presence of the gods.
                                    The Buddha

Overcome anger by non-anger; overcome evil by good; overcome the miser by giving; overcome the liar by truth.
                                    The Buddha

One who controls occurring anger as one would a chariot gone off the track, that one I call a charioteer; other people just hold the reins.
                                    The Buddha

Victory breeds hatred; the defeated sleeps in misery. One who has calmed down sleeps in comfort, having given up victory and defeat.
                                    The Buddha

Do not say anything harsh; what you have said will be said back to you. Angry talk is painful; retaliation will get you.
                                    The Buddha

Let those who have done good repeat it over and over; set your mind on it, for happiness is the accumulation of good.
                                    The Buddha

PHRASES TO MEDITATE ON

(continued)

For those whom are always courteous and respectful of elders, four things increase: life, beauty, happiness, and strength.

The Buddha

Though one defeats a million men in battle, one who overcomes the self alone is in fact the highest victor.

The Buddha

Do not think a small virtue
Will not return in your future lives.
Just as falling drops of water
Will fill a large container,
The little virtues
The steadfast accumulate
Will completely overwhelm them.

The Buddha

It is very foolish and ignorant to retaliate with spite, in the hope of ending the attack of the enemy, because the retaliation itself only brings more suffering.

Chandrakirti

PHRASES TO MEDITATE ON

(continued)

Whatever joy there is in this world,
All comes from desiring others to be happy,
And whatever suffering there is in this world
All comes from desiring myself to be happy.

But what need is there to say much more?
The childish work for their own benefit,
The Buddhas work for the benefit of others.
Just look at the difference between them!
                        Master Shantideva

Live with compassion
Work with compassion
Die with compassion
Meditate with compassion
Enjoy with compassion
When problems come,
Experience them with compassion.
                        Lama Zopa Rinpoche

For as long as space abides
And for as long as sentient beings abide
May I too abide
To dispel the sufferings of sentient beings.
                        Master Shantideva

No matter how many excellent deeds
You may have performed for a thousand eons.
Such as generosity or making offerings to the
Buddhas,
They all perish in one fit of anger.
                        Master Shantideva

PHRASES TO MEDITATE ON

(continued)

There is nothing to trust in seeking happiness from outside; you will only become exhausted from suffering, which is without satisfaction and without end.

Lama Zopa Rinpoche

If you want to know your past life, look into your present condition; if you want to know your future life, look at your present actions.

Padmasambhava

This existence of ours is as transient as autumn clouds
To watch the birth and death of beings is like looking at the movements of a dance.
A lifetime is like a flash of lightning in the sky,
Rushing by, like a torrent down a steep mountain.

Buddha

Even if you donated three hundred pots
Of cooked food three times a day,
It could not compare to even a fraction
Of the merit from just a moment's love.

Nagarjuna

PHRASES TO MEDITATE ON

(continued)

Accumulating wealth, guarding it and making it grow will wear you down; understand that riches bring unending ruin and destruction.

Nagarjuna

When you check your own mind properly, you stop blaming others for your problems. You recognise that your mistaken actions come from your own defiled, deluded mind.

Lama Thubten Yeshe

The human mind has the potential for infinite development. If you can discover, even in a small way, that true satisfaction comes from your mind, you will realise that you can extend this experience without limit and that it is possible to discover everlasting satisfaction.

Lama Thubten Yeshe

All he [Buddha] wanted was for us to understand our own nature. Isn't that so simple? You don't have to believe in anything. Simply by making the right effort, you understand things through your own experience, and gradually develop all realisations.

Lama Thubten Yeshe

ABOUT THE AUTHOR

VENERABLE THUBTEN LHUNDRUP (CHRIS McGLONE)
is a Buddhist monk living at Thubten Shedrup Ling Monastery in Australia.

He has been studying Buddhism for the past eight years, spending much of
that time at Tara Institute in Melbourne, Australia.

Venerable Lhundrup regularly teaches at Atisha Centre, one of the teaching and
meditation centres in the FPMT (Foundation for the Preservation of the
Mahayana Tradition).

Dedication

*May all beings everywhere
Plagued with sufferings of body and mind
Obtain an ocean of happiness and joy
By virtue of my merits*
Master Shantideva